Tending the Soul's Garden

Permaculture as a Way Forward

in Difficult Times

Denise Rushing

Dancing TreePeople Publications,

Lake County, CA

Revised Edition, 2012

PUBLISHED BY DANCING TREEPEOPLE PUBLICATIONS,
UPPER LAKE CALIFORNIA, USA

Copyright © 2011, 2012 by Denise Rushing

Published in the United States
By Dancing TreePeople Publications
www.dancingtreepeople.com

Library of Congress Cataloging-in-Publications Data:
Rushing, Denise , March 28, 2011 revised February 2012
Tending the Soul's Garden / Permaculture as a Way Forward in Dif-
ficult Times / Denise Rushing
Includes bibliographical references.
ISBN 978-0-9835026-0-9

Library of Congress Control Number: 2011926241

To Loretta

Acknowledgements:

Many individuals have influenced me in the writing of this book, many more than I can acknowledge here. Special recognition goes to the following for both who they are and for their contribution:

Thomas Berry and Brian Swimme, for writing *The Universe Story* and for their enduring wisdom;

Fathers of Permaculture and Natural Farming, Bill Mollison, David Holmgren, and Masanobu Fukuoka for their genius in observing nature;

Permaculture Activists and Designers, Benjamin Fahrer, Erik Ohlson, and Starhawk, for their inspiration and instruction;

Renee Shields, for her love and kindness and for her grace in the face of adversity;

My children, Brian and Teresa, who in becoming themselves, amaze me and challenge me to grow;

My partner, Loretta McCarthy, for her editorial eye, unconditional love, encouragement, and insight.

CONTENTS

{ix}

TENDING THE SOUL'S GARDEN

Permaculture as a Way Forward

in Difficult Times

Denise Rushing

Everyone and everything is a
garden. All have to be nurtured,
be they of the forest or the sea.
If we are not gentle with life, the
garden within us dies.

–Song of Waitaha[1]

Creating a Positive Future

In August of 2001, after many years in energy and technology start-up companies, I was a person in spiritual crisis. Even though I was successful in my career, I felt increasingly discouraged by the state of the world and my own trajectory in it. After experiencing increasing panic attacks and chest pains, I realized that I needed to choose a different path.

I left the technology world and moved to rural California, looking for a place to rest and heal. In the months that followed, while I had mitigated the physical symptoms of the crisis I found myself in, I hadn't yet found a new way forward. I explored spiritual traditions and studied the spiritual mystics, all the while looking for ways to "come home" to myself.

In the summer of 2002, I asked myself a question: "What do you want to do with the rest of your life?" That same question invited me to the Masters Degree program at Holy Names University's Sophia Center, a wisdom school centered on Thomas Berry's work in The New Story of the Universe. A few short weeks later, I enrolled in the Sophia Center program.

Many seeds were planted during my time at the Sophia Center, and many more were tended and watered and fed in such a way that I was filled with an excitement, awe and curiosity for engaging in what Thomas Berry calls "the Great Work of our time": societal and cultural transformation. While at the Center, it was as if my soul was being nourished and fed. I deepened the understanding that transformation was necessary if humans were to rediscover their love for Earth and enter into a mutually beneficial relationship with our planet home. I grew increasingly aware of my own role in this work and I learned that in order to find my own path, I needed to pause and pay attention to the energies within me and in my various relationships: both human and nonhuman. I learned to just "be" and from a deep internal place, I discovered what it was I wanted to do next. Intuitively, I knew it would involve ecological gardening or farming, and this gave me a renewed energy and focus.

Soon after my studies, I encountered the practice of *permaculture,* (**perm**anent agri-**culture**) also known as *regenerative design* or *ecological design.* Here was a way to put my emerging cosmology into practice! With great passion, I devoted the next years to learning permaculture and becoming more proficient.

I applied my permaculture design practice first to the garden and then to our farm. I found that as I worked to transform the garden, the garden was also transforming me. Thus, the same permaculture approach was valuable to my own personal evolution, and eventually to my work in community, organizational and governmental structures. I discovered that if I aligned my personal energies with natural forces, rather than fighting them, the work became deeply satisfying and ultimately created even greater abundance.

Permaculture became a way to engage in

the world while at the same time engaging in a process of soul tending, or "gardening the soul." I gradually experienced the two as connected.

As each of us engages in difficult work, we risk becoming depleted and disillusioned for there is so much work to do as powerful forces support the continued plundering of the planet's diverse community of life and human communities. Returning to the principles of permaculture time and again, we can engage in a way that is life giving, renewing and satisfying. For myself, and many others, permaculture has become both a spiritual practice and a positive way of engaging in the world: a way of life.

This book is a brief introduction to applied permaculture and how it can help us engage in difficult and sometimes overwhelming work with a sense of balance, hope and purpose. In it, I hope to share the gentle and hopeful practice of permaculture, as applied to human communities and the human spirit, with the hope that others might use these tools to create a positive future for themselves and those around them.

The Great Work now...
is to carry out the transition
from a period of human
devastation of the Earth to a
period where humans would
be present to the planet in a
mutually beneficial manner.[2]

--*Thomas Berry*

Chapter One

Everything is a Garden, Everything

Gardens

The State of Our World

We are alive at an amazing and difficult time. No other human generation has experienced a time such as this: where humans around the globe are both connected and facing the horrifying reality that the entire planet is in peril. Earth herself is approaching the end of a geo-biological age, with the extinction of life taking place at a rate unseen in 65 million years and we are the human witnesses to this profound event.

Our response? We scurry about our lives, checking wristwatches, buying plastic patio furniture, and listening to cable news stories about the latest celebrity drama. All the while, a whole age of diversity and life and astonishing creation is coming to an end. What's worse, we, as a species, are the primary cause of this destruction! Collectively, we do not seem to know what to do, maintaining a seemingly mindless denial. At times we feel so disconnected from what is happening that we no longer seem to care.

Yet, we *do* care. As part of this planet earth, we feel this change in our bones. Some seek solace in entertainment, material goods, all kinds of addictions, and even religious pursuits, finding it difficult to face the reality of our circumstance. Meanwhile, animals retreat from our subdivisions and mall parking lots. Tragically, many leave Earth forever—some for lack of habitat, some meeting their end in their encounter with our machines on our roads, and some whole species die mysteriously as if to say: *I have had enough of this.*

The diversity of life on Earth, this wonderful, fascinating part of our soul, is in trouble. In our longing for connection to nature, we simulate the thrill of that connection by buying SUVs and outdoor toys, ripping up the hillsides in our quest. In the meantime, further economic downturn and even the potential collapse of our human economy, our human community and our natural world, looms like a dark storm cloud in the distance.

Today, many of us are awakening to this difficulty and seek authentic connection—to others and to the natural world. These moments of truth give us pause, for we no sooner deepen connection than our increased sensitivity brings us into grief over the state of our world. So we disengage and in doing so, further perpetuate the destructive cycle.

How might we remain engaged and aware of the pain of our world and still act out of a deep insight and compassion? How can we maintain optimism in these times? How might we offer a sense of purpose and hope to our children? How might we be *fully alive* and *fully present* in the face of such difficulty? Even the questions can lead to difficulty and sometimes even despair.

One Candle

In February 2003, on the eve of the Iraq war, I felt this despair keenly. It was as if we were all hurtling toward destruction, on autopilot. That night, I joined with a dozen or so friends in a candlelight vigil. It seemed the decision to go to war had already been made but not yet announced and people were amassing along the street corners and public places with candles. We joined millions around the globe in a candlelight prayer for peace.

I held my candle aloft into the dark night sky from the balcony above the Oakland Hills and wondered: "How could my one candle stop this senseless war?" I held it as a prayer, in fervent hope that seemed so utterly hopeless. The forces were building, a whole people would soon feel our country's shock and awe... and my weapon of defiance and hope?

A candle.

I held the candle aloft. The act seemed so futile. Soon after that night, more and more, I was noticing the destruction of our world and was fighting this ever-present feeling of despair. I read that Eskimos were concerned about the Arctic caribou and seal as the glaciers shrank. I sat next to a gentleman on an airplane who was playing an army-produced desert storm war game on his Dell Latitude. He carried a virtual AK47 and hand grenades, drove tanks and all-terrain vehicles. He shot at anything that moved. The screen was littered with bodies... but the bodies melted quickly into clean desert landscape so as to not clutter the game with their mess. The lady across the aisle thumbed through SkyMall magazine. She could dial 1-800-skymall to have closet organizers delivered directly to her door.

I was also aware that thousands of Americans and hundreds of thousands of Iraqis would die in a war that would cost our country billions or even trillions. Teachers in California could no longer receive a tax credit for buying school supplies for their classrooms. The entire state of California was going broke. Everywhere I looked, all I saw was humans in denial and our species in decline.

My candle seemed so small.

Yet, in the face of this apparently overwhelming feeling of despair, I still dreamed. I imagined a day when billions of candles lit the night, when we collectively awakened from our insane binge to fully engage our most talented in the work of renewal and resurrection and reconstruction and justice for human and non-human life.

Somewhere in the increasing depths of hopelessness, I imagined this. And then it dawned on me: *even a single small candle can light a room.*

Determined to keep my own candle lit in what seemed to me to be an ever-growing dark-ness, I decided to cultivate my own well being so that I could engage in what Thomas Berry called "The Great Work of our time"-- the work of cultural transformation and, as it turns out, a transformational inner journey. In that process of committing to action over despair, I found the energies to cultivate gratitude in myself and, like nutrients in a garden, this commitment pre-pared the soil of my inner garden for the seeds to come., including the seed of permaculture.

What is Permaculture?

At first look, permaculture, also known as regenerative design or ecological agriculture, is an ecologically-based design system which allows us to improve our relationship with the land by observing and imitating nature, while using and integrating natural systems and methods rather than fighting against them. Permaculture ethics, intentions and principles are those of nature herself, and can be applied to the garden, the farm, and indeed any living system including human structures.

However, in practice, permaculture also cultivates a way of being that tends to go much deeper than simply a system of ecological design. Somehow, by engaging with nature in intimate observation, we gradually become a part of the system and magically and necessarily engage in our own evolution and transformation. In fact, the ethics, principles, and roots of permaculture practice, can go far beyond the garden or farm and into the invisible structures of our relationships with ourselves and others, as well as our community and organizational structures. By engaging in permaculture, one soon and eagerly applies the approach to other complex systems and challenges.

One of the key tenets of permaculture is

relationship. Everything gardens. In an actual garden, this is easy to observe, over time. Every element in a garden, whether it is a plant, an insect, a rock, a pond, animals, a tree or a structure, has an effect on the others. The effect, in most cases, is predictable just by observing the nature of the element placed.

For example, here in Northern California, a large rock in a garden covers the soil preserving moisture, creates habitat for frogs and lizards, provides shade at certain times of the day, and may even create a microclimate for some plants. The rock, *by its very being, its relationships and its placement,* is gardening. It might be fair to say that we, like the rock, need simply find our appropriate place and relationships to create a beneficial impact. Also, like the rock, we might have a detrimental impact if we are not in the appropriate relationships or place.

So, permaculture offers a way to engage with the world on a small scale, while keeping in mind a vision for the larger design. This is how nature works: a set of laws or principles, such as gravity or atomic bonding, are true for all natural systems. By varying relationship

ETHICAL
INTENTION

PRINCIPLES

ROOTS OF THE
PRACTICE

and scale, the same elemental building blocks evolve into many diverse, intelligent, systems— systems that begin as small experiments evolve or sometime burst into being a myriad of successful co-creative regenerative ecosystems.

By studying and then understanding how systems work and especially how they change, I found that I was able to accept that I was doing my part. By doing what I did well and and what brought me joy, I found greater energy for the work. Paradoxically, by focusing on small solutions, I found meaning and purpose even in the face of the larger destruction around me.

Permaculture as A Framework

Permaculture provides a design framework for empowerment and action –cultivating inner wisdom and gifts, honoring the wisdom of nature and engaging in the world as nature does—with the desire to be a part of the natural rhythms and cycles, cooperating with the whole of the natural world. The permaculture framework includes the following aspects:

Ethical Intention: what is important, true or right relationship;

Roots: regular practices that balance being and doing;

Principles: How to engage, with nature as teacher and guide.

If we symbolically illustrate the aspects of permaculture using a tree, the branches, leaves and fruit of the tree represent the abundance of the tree, or what it produces in each cycle of seasons: the ethical intention come to life. The tree's roots cannot be seen above ground, and yet are vital to the life of the tree, bringing nutrients from the soil to feed the life of the tree and enable it to grow. And the trunk represents that point of transition, where the nutrients are transformed and given to the tree for its life-giving processes.

These aspects of permaculture; ethical intention, roots of the practice, and principles, are described briefly here and in greater detail in the chapters that follow.

The *ethical intention* of permaculture is the vision of what we would like to produce: *abundance.* Our intention is *ethical,* in that it is larger than us, creates good benefit for others and for earth. The *intention* is our vision or dream of an ultimate design or result.

The *roots of the practice* are the permaculture practices that allow us to observe and analyze the entire system and to approach the design as nature does.

The roots represent the way we are, allowing nature to work, allowing ourselves to be, cultivating our gifts and our inner life, and using observation to notice the way things work, the state of our relationships, how the energies work in a garden, a community or in ourselves. The roots are all about being present, going into darkness to find the relationships and nutrients the system needs to thrive.

The *principles of permaculture* are a framework for action—translating the way we are into the action we must take to manifest our intention. This translation from being to doing is at the heart of mystery—a point that translates intention and being into decision and focussed action. This is represented as a cycle, like breathing: from being to doing and back again.

In the sections that follow, we will explore each of these aspects of permaculture with a view of both living gardens: the visible external gardens and the invisible realm and structures: such as community, and the internal garden of the soul. We do this with the intention of cultivating our capacity to engage in the work ahead with a sense of purpose and hope.

Tending the Soul's Garden

Inspiration is not garnered
from the litanies of what may
befall us; it resides in humanity's
willingness to restore, redress,
reform, rebuild, recover,
reimagine, and reconsider.

--Paul Hawken

Chapter Two

Ethical Intention

Statements of Ethical Intention

Permaculture starts with ethical intention. The three statements of ethical intention for the practice of permaculture are:

Care of Earth: All life systems have the provisions and resources to continue and thrive.

Care of People: All people have the provisions to access the resources necessary for their existence.

"Fair share" or **Return the Surplus**: We set limits to consumption by taking only what we need, and by governing our own needs so that resources are set aside for Earth and others. [3]

The ethical intention is a statement of our most significant primary relationships and in some sense, what "right" or "good" relationship can be. The ethical intention of permaculture is the conscious dream, or the desired fruit of our work. We imagine the world as we would like it to be.

Underlying this deepest intention of permaculture, is a personal *decision* or commitment to *take responsibility for our own existence and that of future generations.* [3]

This decision is profound, and by making it, we find inner resources and give ourselves permission to learn and grow. By this commitment, to take responsibility for our own existence and that of future generations, we begin with a decision for our own existence.

We, thus, must begin this journey with ourselves: our own inner being, inner authority, inner wisdom and deepest emotions, dreams and desires. In this ethical intention, we, by necessity, first open ourselves to a path of self-knowledge and growth.

The ethical intention can be reframed, as we look deeper into our own personal well being through self-care: care of body, care of relationships, including self-relationship, and offering our abundant gifts to others and ourselves.

The gifts that emerge from this, our inner garden, can be extraordinary.

"The only ethical decision is to take responsibility for our own existence and that of our children. Make it now." [4]

--Bill Mollison

Permaculture as a Path

Permaculture, then, is a path—a design for living in a complex changing system. It is a way to engage completely and with full awareness, with a sense of purpose and optimism, and with an understanding that small actions, actions that feel like play and bring us joy, are vital to the whole. We know we are aligned and are on the path when we feel that sense of joy, interest and life-giving purpose.

As we engage in this way we learn from and work with and within nature, pay greater attention to both our inner and outer world, and, in doing so, create abundance.

Choosing Life

To begin this journey, we must necessarily start with self-examination: what brings us life?

A decade ago, I wondered why it was that I did not have "a dream" for my life. So many that I admired that had large dreams: Martin Luther King for Civil Rights, Harvey Milk for Gay Rights, Brian Swimme for the Universe

Story or almost any dedicated artist for their art. It seemed to me that I had plenty of talents and gifts, but nothing that led me to that level of single-minded focused passion.

On Martin Luther King's birthday in 2003 I was asked to write my own version of his "*I Have a Dream*" speech and share that dream with others. I was brought to tears, wondering, "What *is* my Dream?" In examining this upwelling of emotion, I awoke to the fear within me and the realization that I was afraid to dream. It wasn't that I didn't have a dream, but rather my dream was so huge that it seemed well beyond my individual capability to realize. It was as if I dared not speak it aloud, let alone dream it!

So I made a choice: I would speak it aloud that day. Since that time, I have found that this dream, a vision of right relationship with Earth and each other, has been guiding my life:

I imagine a day when we collectively
awaken to fully engage together in the
work of renewal, restoration and justice for
human communities and the web of life.

To create a vision with intention, we must awaken to what wants to live within us. We might start with the following question: "What brings me energy and passion?" or "What is it I most want?" or even "What brings me life?" By exploring these questions, we can imagine what fulfilling our vision would be like. Our individual imagination brings forth the gift of visioning or dreaming about the future. Through our imagination, we can choose the future we wish to create together—our ethical intention. Along the way, we will need the energies of life to overcome barriers and make hard choices. We can choose to dwell in fear and cynicism or instead commit to and imagine a future of ever-increasing abundance, and of life.

Imagination is a key nutrient in creating a permaculture design for a garden. In fact, imagination may also be one of the most important internal resources in creating possibilities for our lives. As permaculture designers, we choose to discover our dreams and make them a conscious vision and intention rather than an unconscious fear.

"The Dream Drives the Action." [5]

One of the best examples of a conscious dream driving the action of an entire community took place in Clearlake Oaks, California. In the fifties, this community, known to locals as "The Oaks," was a vacation spot. Over time, the cabins and homes deteriorated, and by the mid-nineties, meth labs and drug houses occupied the center of the town. Pastor Bill Thornton and his wife Ruth Canady of the United Methodist Church surveyed the landscape with one of their parishioners and asked "What do you see here?"

The parishioner shrugged as he looked across the center of town and said—"I see desperation and drugs and blight. I see all these problems that are almost impossible for our community to solve. We are afraid to walk here at night."

"That's not what I see," said Thornton. He went on to describe his vision: a thriving community center, a plaza where the community gathers and celebrates, where children play, a community that loves and cares for one another, and a church where all are welcome. "I see us celebrating together in this plaza."

In the months and years that followed, local citizens, the business community, the local governmental agencies and the churches all worked toward fulfilling that dream. Citizens volunteered, designed, and donated the money to build a park. The redevelopment agency designed and constructed a new plaza. The church opened a thrift store and is now working on a youth center. Citizens started the nearby Clarks Island Sustainability Initiative involving youth and the entire community. Where there was once blight, a joyful transformation took place, and continues to this day, fueled by that initial visionary dream.

In less than a decade, the community held its Grand Opening of its town plaza. As the citizens gathered to celebrate, and children played in the plaza, the community honored the late Pastor Thornton and their entire community of Clearlake Oaks by re-telling this story and proclaiming: "Look what love has done!"

Natural farming is not just for growing crops, it is for the cultivation and perfection of human beings. [6]

--*Masanobu Fukuoka, The One Straw*

Revolution

Chapter Three

Noticing: The Roots of Permaculture

Practice

Start with the Soil

Gardeners often say, "start with the soil." And this is true of any endeavor, be it garden, farm or our own inner well being. Why do we start with the soil? In a garden, the health of the garden plants and trees depends upon the health of the soil. Is it balanced? Does it have nutrients? Is it filled with beneficial life? Is the structure of the soil life-giving? Tending the soil in a garden can be a metaphor for tending our inner spiritual life, tending the inner life for new creativity, generation and abundance.

Soil has a story and bears the history of all that has happened to it, and so do we. Soil can be brought into balance and health, and so can we. Unless we understand the soil, we will not have a productive garden over time—the health of the soil establishes the possibilities that follow.

Returning to our analogy of the tree, the soil supports the nourishment of the tree. The roots of the tree take up nutrients, water from the soil and, with sunlight, transform these into abundance. These roots go deep into the soil for what they need. The symbiotic relationship between the organisms in the soil and the roots of the plants help both to thrive. And so it is with the roots of our permaculture practice. The roots help us to enrich the soil of our own being while providing us with insight and inspiration as creative designers. We create abundance as we take up the nourishment we need.

We begin by nurturing the soil: the soil of the soul and in the various gardens we tend in our lives. Soil is where life begins: and the cycle of life continues. Infused with spirit, the archetypal soil of mother earth brings us to a new way of being, transforming our world as an outward expression of our inner journey.

The Roots of Permaculture Practice

THOUGHTFUL
AND PROTRACTED
OBSERVATION

WHOLE SYSTEMS
THINKING

SMALL AND SLOW
SOLUTIONS, OR "START
SMALL THEN EXPAND"

Paying Attention

These root practices are like the roots of a tree. The first root practice, thoughtful and protracted observation, as applied to the garden, allows us to see where the energies flow—sun, wind, rain, birds, human traffic. Over time, we notice patterns.

The dimension of time, often not appreciated in our culture of instant information and gratification, is used by nature and evolution to a startling effect. Time wears away mountains, changes the course of rivers, evolves stars into humans... and within us, time brings growth, change, and awareness. Depending upon our choices and our circumstances, time transforms us and can bring about bitterness or healing, apathy or living fully, a cynical certitude or a deeper, gentler wisdom.

Thoughtful and protracted observation creates awareness, which creates the conditions for evolution and transformation of a garden. In our internal landscape, simply by noticing energy flows and our internal conditions, awareness gradually surfaces, and with it comes clarity.

For example, one of my own experiences of this took place shortly after I began farming. At first, I found farm life to be simple and satisfying, interrupted by my own perceived crusades from which I frequently found I needed to learn balance, rhythm and being. My first teacher was a noxious weed: Star Thistle.

Star Thistle populates ground that has been abused: dry, compacted, or scraped clean. In Northern California, this invasive weed is often found next to the highway and can be identified by its characteristic prickly star head as it reaches maturity. The points are so sharp that they pierce leather gloves and most clothing (ouch!)

While Star Thistle had not claimed our entire orchard, it had overtaken a large portion of the backyard and a few other orchard locations. I noticed that this thistle gained a foothold in places that had seen a bulldozer blade in the preceding few years.

My first impulse was to enter full-scale battle with this weed and I immediately began to fret and worry about how it could be done. I noticed that my neighbor mowed and sprayed herbicides and rototilled the ground. His approach not only seemed time consuming and expensive, but it went against my desire to work with nature rather than constantly fighting natural systems. His methods required constant vigilance and his yard had more star thistle than mine, so his approach did not seem to work well in the end.

At first, fueled with zeal and a competitive spirit, I went after the star thistle in a weed-pulling frenzy. At the end of the first few days, I was sore and exhausted and the star thistle still seemed to be everywhere--popping into full bloom and most certainly re-seeding itself. I quickly realized that I needed to find a different way to interact with this plant; my energy toward it seemed counter-productive. So I decided to observe the start thistle for a while, and attempted to think about ways that I could enjoy it.

How could I possibly enjoy this plant? It grew faster than all the others, and with no water or care, could quickly dominate an area. After some thoughtful observation, I realized that

it had a job to do and was quite successful at doing it. If I were to remove the start thistle, I would have to find a more successful and faster way to do its job: repairing the dry, hard ground and creating soil structure where there currently was none. I noticed where it grew, how easy or difficult it was to pull out depending upon the circumstances it found itself in, how it sprouted if I didn't get the tap-root out, how it re-sprouted if left on the ground after it was pulled and how all the thistles opened even as it was dying. If I could not enjoy it, I could certainly admire its tenacity!

With even more observation, I noticed that star thistle did not grow where we had mulched with straw. I also noticed that the whole plant came out easily if the ground was watered the night before but pulled before the plant had a chance to soften to the new water.

I began to enjoy the time spent observing and continued to observe even while I was pulling out the star thistle. I found that I enjoyed the satisfaction of working small sections of the garden, where whole plants came out easily after watering, and found that I was no longer worried about the entire yard. I decided that we will have many seasons together, the star thistle and I, and that eventually, with my help, the soil would someday be moist and healthy and no longer in need of this weed.

I also noticed an internal shift. I noticed that, in some ways, I had been like star thistle: tenacious, hearty, energetic and strong. Heroic even. Now I knew that I must cultivate a deeper nature in myself: gentle, patient, and enjoying the smaller, simpler task of working the soil. With enough gentle care and cultivation, I was growing increasingly aware that new life would emerge in my inner garden as well.

Whole Systems Thinking

The second root practice of *whole systems thinking* centers on relationship and connection. Everything is connected to everything else in some way, shape or form. In the garden, noticing these relationships and planning for them or designing them into a system helps the garden "garden" itself.

The same can be said for less visible structures. Whether it is a family, government, organization or community, understanding the relationships between the various energies and elements in the system can provide valuable insights.

For the inner landscape, self-understanding can be gained in a variety of ways and each element of the system is related. Cultivating a greater understanding of the whole system is possible by looking to understand any one element.

For example, my partner Loretta and I decided to improve our nutrition by entering into a 28 day "cleanse" where we avoided caffeine, sugar, gluten, dairy and other potential allergens and then reintroduced them one at a time at the end of the month. We expected that we would face some minor emotional issues as well as physical adaptations when we embarked on this exercise, so to make it easier, we decided to cook delicious and colorful meals each day and make a point of eating them at the table together. We avoided eating out, or on the run, and we stayed true to the program the entire time. In this process, we noticed that this one aspect of ourselves, our "food intake," profoundly affected the whole system of our personal well being and our life together.

We each were surprised at the extent and the impact of this one change. It not only impacted our feelings more than we expected, but it profoundly and positively impacted our respective energy levels, our relationship, and our involvement in our hobbies, our time together and even our willingness to take on new projects. For my part, I was surprised to discover that I had been relying on snacks to deaden strong feelings I had regarding difficulties I faced. Through this one change, I began feeling those powerful and difficult feelings and I had the energy to make needed changes.

To see everything as connected is both an underlying belief and a way to observe and notice the world around us. Nature moves in concert—pull one thread in the web of life and others respond to take advantage, adapt or perish. The act of noticing, in itself, nourishes our creative spirit.

Start Small

The third root practice is to start small then expand or consider small and slow solutions. In the garden, on the farm and in life, we can avoid unrecoverable regrettable major errors by trying things out and by implementing on a small scale first. If we implement in phases, with an understanding of our actions and an awareness of the actual scale and scope of a project, we can save resources, pain and heartache later.

Using small and slow solutions minimizes risk, and the likelihood of a negative reaction. It helps to remember that every action causes a reaction. Most people learn this lesson the hard way. In our zeal to implement our newly learned technical skills, and our desire to design to a larger scale, we sometimes make mistakes that cannot be corrected, mistakes that live on long after we made them. The unrecoverable errors are known as "Class One Errors" in permaculture circles, and they almost always happen as a result of creating something too large too quickly.

For example before undertaking any project that requires significant investment in a garden like building a structure or creating a pond, it would be wise to test the idea or implement it on a smaller scale. We might layout the outline, and observe: does the new pond negatively impact the flow of foot traffic on site? Would the newly planted tree shade the only sunny garden area?

The inner landscape can be impacted by regrettable errors as well. Human recovery is possible, of course, but in these, the choice has a lasting impact that might be avoided with more careful consideration up front.Examples include: choosing a course of study outside of our own interests in order to please others, allowing others to make choices for us that have a lasting effect on our own well-being, or significant financial investment mistakes.

By starting small then expanding, many regrettable errors can be avoided. In addition to avoiding mistakes, small scale and slow solutions offer key benefits in a time of change because many solutions can be developed simultaneously by many different people on a smaller scale, with less cost and risk. Successful solutions will grow quickly, with increasing energies, while others may languish.

Whole systems undergo transformation through evolution, which is a series of both small and slow solutions and major, sometimes more violent, advancements in the face of crises. Yet, even in crises, the seeds of the future "large" solution were often in the background for some time before coming to the fore. Small-scale solutions give a system time to adapt, to see and imagine the bigger change, and then the change requires less effort to accomplish.

Noticing Patterns, Large to Small

Nature works in patterns, from simple to increasingly complex. Larger scale patterns are often composed of smaller versions of that same pattern. For example, fractals on a miniature scale predict the nature of the larger design and vice versa. By cultivating an awareness of and noticing patterns in nature or in our human systems, we can invest our energies wisely on a small scale and still have confidence that the smaller scale solutions will apply to larger scale problems *if* the concept resonates and its time has come.

One example of this takes place every day in the online social networking circles. Why is it that some videos easily go viral and others do not? Why is it that some Facebook trends take off and others don't? In many cases of truly far-reaching, thoughtful or culture changing content, the author did not set out to make a video that would receive a million views or a post that would change the world. While the author might have larger scale change in mind, more often than not, they began by creating something that spoke powerfully to their own smaller connected community.

Thus, the online social network, as a virtual medium, works as nature does. Word travels quickly through millions or even billions of individual decisions and actions to share information, insights or ideas. Almost all of these start small. The underlying reality is this: as in nature, smaller patterns are a reflection of greater ones. In this case, individual ideas that resonate, coupled with individual decision-making, can result in an effective local action.

Local action, multiplied many times, can create global change.

Similarly, patterns often repeat themselves in nature and in human systems, particularly our inner garden. Noticing repeating patterns in nature allows us to start small and then grow our design as nature might. Noticing repeating patterns in our own relationships, interactions or emotions can lead to powerful, often life-changing, insights.

Nature does not hurry, yet

everything is

accomplished.

–Lao Tzu

Chapter Four

Nature as Teacher and Guide

The Principles of Permaculture

The Principles of Permaculture

In Chapter One, we introduced the concept that everything is a garden and everything gardens. This suggests that we can apply permaculture--natural principles and practices-- to anything, garden, farm, community or individual human being. We learned that approaching problems as nature does offers us a way to move forward with meaning and purpose in the face of difficulty.

In Chapter Two, we touched on the importance of ethical intention: of commitment, of *deciding to act* and thus aligning with natural energies.

In Chapter Three, we introduced the *roots* of permaculture practice, which are ways of being and observing, but not yet engaging in action. We learned that the roots reach into the nutrients of the soil for nourishment and that the abundance depends upon the renewal of those nutrients.

We now turn to the mysterious point of transformation, the point where the tree's roots enter the trunk of the tree and intention and nourishment transform into action and abundance.

From our nourishment and inner being, we yearn to create. In this act of creation, we participate with the natural world and thus co-create, or co-evolve. The *principles of permaculture* are particularly valuable in focusing our creative energies.

For many human beings, one of the most difficult challenges of life on Earth during these difficult times is maintaining optimism in the face of difficulty. Key to this is overcoming the sense of isolation and the thought-pattern that the effort of one person doesn't really matter.

By keeping in mind "*start small then expand*", I have found great hope in seeing where the energies of others join my own for an even greater effect.

The following *principles of permaculture*

have been particularly valuable in aligning individual personal energies with others to create beneficial change. These principles were developed over many years by many permaculture designers. They take on a multitude of forms as unique as the people who practice them. Japanese farmer, Masanobu Fukuoka, and Australian permaculturists, Bill Mollison and David Holmgren, developed early, detailed thoughtful observations regarding how nature works and documented these observations. The set of principles included here have developed from the principles they put forth and have been further refined by Northern California permaculture instructors: Benjamin Fahrer, Penny Livingston Stark, and Starhawk among others.

These principles were developed through collaborative, thoughtful and protracted human observation of how nature works over time.

Principles of Permaculture

1. Work with and within nature
2. The problem is an opportunity
3. Least change for the greatest possible effect
4. Relinquish power
5. Relative location
6. Stack functions
7. Energy cycling
8. Stability through beneficial connections
9. Succession of evolution
10. Edge effect
11. Information as a resource
12. Yield of the system is theoretically unlimited
13. Unknown good benefit

Principle 1

Work With and Within Nature

Work with, and within, nature means cooperating with nature and being a part of nature rather than separate from it. It means working with the natural systems, elements, forces, processes, and evolutions, rather than against them. It means becoming a part of the natural systems. We do this so that we can assist rather than impede natural developments. Examples include the use of natural biological elements like farm animals to increase soil fertility, taking advantage of gravity, incorporating the energies of the sun and wind, and encouraging native species.

Working *with* nature involves observation and learning to understand how nature works. It means *allowing* rather than forcing, and designing so that nature will naturally do the work. Working *within* nature starts with the understanding that we are a part of the system, and can be beneficial, and that we have a role: participating in the cycles of ever-increasing abundance.

In practice, this is one of the more difficult principles of permaculture. As modern humans, we tend to change nature to suit our needs rather than changing our ways to fit into and cultivate natural patterns and systems. Further, we tend to value *making something happen* rather than creating the right conditions and then *allowing something to emerge* as nature might. In some ways, this behavior on our part is indicative of a deeper challenge within our psyche: a fundamental lack of trust that good will emerge, given the right conditions.

Principle 2

The Problem is an Opportunity

The problem is an opportunity means that within each problem are the seeds of opportunity. We are only limited by the way we look at a "problem" and by our imagination. By changing our way of seeing the problem, we also allow ourselves to think differently and more creatively. Implicit in this principle is the understanding that everything works both ways. It is only how we look at something that makes it advantageous or not: anything and everything can be a positive resource.

For example, when I took on a older walnut orchard and converted it to organic production, I faced a huge problem brought about by monoculture farming: namely the walnut trees create a substance called juglone that prevents photosynthesis in many plants. I believed that this would prevent me from creating successful gardens anywhere near the walnut trees.

What was the opportunity in this? Juglone would be in the soil for years, even if a tree were removed. Initially, I saw this as a huge problem. I had imagined creating beautiful and abundant farm-scale permaculture food forests with a wide variety of plants, many of whom would not enjoy juglone in the soil. The seeds of opportunity in this problem were elusive.

This particular problem required that I make friends with the idea of older walnut trees and see the process of caring for and cultivating the orchard as a long term one. I researched plants that tolerate juglone well, I found uses for older less productive trees, and I befriended the idea of trying things out on a much smaller scale. In the end, the orchard is what it is--a lot of older walnut trees. The opportunity is this: slow down, learn how to garden using raised beds and juglone-tolerant plants. In fact, grasses and grains are juglone-tolerant and there happens to be a greater opportunity in these than vegetable food forests in our locale, something

I may not have discovered had I not looked for the opportunity.

Given the number and scale of problems facing our communities, understanding the opportunity within each problem becomes an important skill.

Principle 3

Least Change for the Greatest Possible Effect

Least change for the greatest possible effect is also known as leverage, or conservation of energies. The idea is that, through thoughtful design, work becomes a source and not a sink for our energies. We find ways to leverage all energies for the most positive effect

"Energies" in a system can be actual electrical or fuel-based energy (electricity, gasoline, etc.), resources (money, time, garden seeds), more individual energies such as our personal thoughts, love and attention, or societal energies, including organizational efforts, political capital and influence. Every element in the garden or in our lives is chosen and placed or applied for energy efficiency. This principle of *least change for the greatest possible effect* allows permaculture designers to leverage their energies and create significant positive impact with the least amount of effort.

Out of all the principles, this one may have most impacted my life. It allowed me to effectively prioritize my time, a non-renewable resource, so that I could make a difference without becoming depleted. It also allowed me to see where I could best support the work of others. For example, in our communities on the north shore of Clear Lake, I noticed that the same set of volunteers were doing all of the work in almost any local project. I observed that the least change for the greatest effect would be to find a way to cultivate new energies and new volunteers in each of the communities. Two ideas were born out of this realization.

The first was to host town hall meetings where information was shared, the community gathered to celebrate and reflect and learn, and sign-up sheets were circulated where individuals could learn more about what interested them. The second was creating visible and fun projects where anyone traveling by could stop and participate. Both of these approaches have resulted in many new volunteers and even some new leaders in each of our communities.

Principle 4

Relinquish Power

Relinquishing power means that the role of the gardener, as a beneficial authority, is to return function and responsibility to life and people.

In the garden, this can be as simple as giving responsibility for weeding and mulching to a set of low growing ground cover plants. In our inner world, it can take the form of allowing our conscious ego to *serve* our true "soul" self rather than dominating the decision-making. This can be a truly profound shift of trusting intuition, inner wisdom, paying attention to where energies are flowing in oneself and where they are not, paying attention to the unconscious through dreams or an awareness of our attraction to certain archetypal stories.

Returning function "to life" means designing in and allowing for the natural living systems to perform as many of the functions as possible: cleaning water and air among the most important.

Returning function "to people" means that community leaders, whether they be official or unofficial, understand that they are in service to the community and that their primary role is to find a way to empower individuals and their community to become more self-reliant.

Thus, to be the gardener, one releases the idea of controlling a situation and instead sees oneself as cultivating or serving the greater design: to be a *beneficial authority* is to be of service.

Principle 5

Relative Location

Relative Location is cultivating awareness in the placement of elements relative to one another. This awareness of the relationship between elements and their interconnectedness is the key to good design.

This principle highlights the importance of *relationship* in permaculture. Elements are related to one another, have an effect on one another and must not be considered in isolation.

Relative location requires that we also think carefully about the larger design so that major elements are not poorly placed when considering our future plans.

One example of the positive effect of relative location often used in permaculture is in the placement of an herb garden near the kitchen, so that fresh herbs are easily harvested and used in meals. Another is in considering the placement of a tree relative to gardens and shade structures and animals so that the shade, the windbreak and other attributes of the tree help the other elements.

A more metaphorical example of this is in an individual's life, where the elements might be actual human relationships, or life elements, such as job, family, volunteer work, and interests. In this, relative location has more to do with the relationships of these elements with one another—not only in real distance and time, but also in how the items are placed relative to a person's energy flow. Is it difficult to switch from one to another or are they seamlessly integrated? In our modern world, the concept of *relative location* might offer a powerful approach to work-life balance.

Principle 6

Stack Functions

When we *stack functions* we design a system so that *each element performs as many functions as possible.* Each resource is carefully chosen and placed so that it can do this. *Also, each important function needs to be supported by many elements.* In the garden, farm and household, this means that important basic needs such as water, food, energy and fire protection are designed to be supported in two or more ways. In the inner landscape, an element such as keeping a journal can support many functions. It can be a way to unwind, to record events, thoughts, feelings and dreams, or even a way of cultivating creativity through a sense of play.

In a community project, the concept of stacking functions can be useful when considering which organizations or individuals might learn, who might donate resources or where to find sources of funding. For example, a recent tule wetland restoration project on Clarks Island was developed for many reasons: (1) creating beneficial environmental impact, (2) involving local schools in environmental education, (3) initiating a new training program for other similar efforts around Clear Lake, (4) creating a way to galvanize community volunteers, (5) restoring an island park to its natural state and (6) involving local tribes in a cooperative effort.

The natural processes of the tule plants themselves provide an even better example of stacking functions. Tules provide homes for wildlife, inhibit shore erosion, prevent the encroachment of invasive species, clean the waters of the lake through both aeration and nutrient removal, and provide raw materials for the historic activities of local native cultures such as the construction of canoes, shelters and baskets.

Principle 7

Energy Cycling

Energy cycling means paying attention to the flow of energy within a system and optimizing the cyclical or renewable nature of these energies. In a garden or household, good design uses incoming natural energies with those generated on-site to ensure a complete energy cycle.

Permaculture designers aspire to stop the flow of nutrient and energy off the site and instead turn these flows into cycles so that the energy can be renewed and reused again and again.

In the garden, the benefits of this are obvious. Energy and resource inputs can be expensive, so recycling the "energies" of the garden, whether they be nutrients or water, results in less resource use and cost.

How does this principle apply to the human being? It helps to look at our own energy resources as renewable and nonrenewable. As mentioned earlier, time is non-renewable, but with enough sleep, strong relationships, good nutrition and proper cultivation and addition of "soul" nutrients (as discussed in Chapter Six), we can count on renewed daily energies for our work. Notice what activities and relationships renew, engage and create energy, and which of these deplete energy. By paying attention, we are likely to discover daily, monthly and annual cycles and make better choices on not only how to invest our personal energies, but we can also better prepare ourselves for the necessary relationships and activities that deplete them.

Principle 8

Stability Through Beneficial Connections Between Diverse Beings

Stability is achieved through beneficial connections between diverse beings. Thus, diversity is related to stability. It is not, however, the *number* of diverse elements you can pack into a system, but rather the useful or beneficial relationships you can create between these elements.

Stable systems are created through beneficial connections. This suggests that for those who worry about the stability of their household or local economy, or any other significant outer problem for that matter, time might be best spent creating and cultivating beneficial relationships. With these relationships, comes less volatility and greater stability.

Principle 9

Succession of Evolution

Succession of evolution takes place in our inner or outer garden over time and each cycle is an opportunity for more abundance.

As time goes by, systems evolve—and a predictable succession of plant functions or human capacities unfold. As a garden, or any other system for that matter, evolves, the beneficial aspects of that evolution can be enhanced with thoughtful intention and design.

The permaculture designer looks to accelerate natural processes to hasten the development of sustainable, ecologically diverse, and abundant systems. In the garden, this first means that what you do not get to this season, you will have opportunities when the cycle returns. It also means that with each seasonal cycle, as you add elements or make small changes to methods, processes, or relationships, the system will improve over time.

In our individual lives, this is similarly true. With each season, we can invest in and cultivate our relationships, our inner well being, our physical health, our work efforts and our immediate environment. We do not have to solve our problems all at once--we can trust that the cycle will return and that we can take small steps to improve our contribution. An important aspect of this is how we choose to invest our most critical and nonrenewable resources, particularly time.

Succession of evolution allows us to trust *time* as another dimension in our work. Our efforts may not appear to be creating any beneficial change at first. In fact, many permaculture designers work on their soil and perennial plants in the early years and often describe the phenomena of the garden "popping" in the third or fourth year—when all of the intentional design and nutrients fuel significant growth.

Similarly, we may invest in our own community or personal growth and we may not notice changes at first. Initially, beneficial change may be gradual and hardly seem worth the effort. However, given time, we can count on evolution. Like a garden, human beings and their communities evolve in fundamentally predictable ways. Given the proper nutrients and the intention, this can be toward ever-increasing and abundant life.

Principle 10

Edge Effect

Edge Effect refers to that which occurs in a system along its edges. The principle recognizes the use of natural patterns as the basis of design. In nature, the creation of greater edge provides us with a greater surface area, therefore giving us greater production, increased positive relationship opportunities, more places for nature to create and work and evolve, and a greater edge between microclimates.

In invisible structures, such as a societal culture, the edges or margins tend to foster a greater creativity. In our personal inner world, the edges are the places of greatest discomfort and often can be that "creative edge" where we experience the most personal growth.

It helps to observe and notice the "edges" both in our community and in our lives and cultivate a deeper awareness of the gifts present in these areas.

Principle 11

Information as a Resource

In permaculture, *information is the critical potential resource.* Bad information can result in poor design. Good information increases opportunity for good design. Many permaculture designers are information enthusiasts and seek multiple sources of information, both traditional and non-traditional.

Information can come to us in a variety of forms. These days, many of us seek our information on the internet and in this it helps to verify what we find. Sometimes we might overlook the best sources of information in our locale. For example, in our community, we have a number of long-time organic farmers. Seeking out what works in our location, when to plant, who is saving seeds, how to manage local invasive species and pests, and how to best bring goods to market, will save a new farmer or gardener untold years of experimentation and resources.

A good permaculture designer becomes both a good researcher and a good listener!

Principle 12

The Yield of the System is Theoretically Unlimited

The yield of the system is theoretically unlimited means that for any natural system, with each increase in the number of functions performed by the individual resources or elements, and with each increase in the number of beneficial relationships, the yield of the systems increases. Because there are no limits to the number of functions that a resource can perform, or the number of relationships within a system, the yield of the system can increase over time, and theoretically this can go on infinitely as long as the system is cyclical and in balance. Natural systems seek balance. Natural systems that have existed for some time, such as old growth forests, have evolved to a high degree of diversity. Their abundance, or yield, is ever increasing with each cycle. How we define abundance in this case is helpful. For example, an old growth forest produces a myriad of life forms, of food for the life forms that live in balance within the system, and each of these life forms thrives. Thriving and ever-increasing life is a good working definition of abundance in such a system.

For a permaculture garden or human system, the yield of the system depends upon the number of resources, the number of functions each resource performs, and the number of beneficial relationships within the system. In human systems, and especially when considering our own internal well being, the same definition of abundance could apply: thriving and ever-increasing life.

The number of functions that any resource performs is only limited by the imagination of the designer or the information available to him or her. Thus both information and imagination are critical aspects to cultivate in any system, including our own internal garden.

Principle 13

Unknown Good Benefit

Unknown good benefit is a statement of trust in a beneficial Universe: if we start out with positive ethical intention, dream or vision, we trust that energies will flow toward our work and other good things follow.

This principle requires that we are first clear and honest about our intention for any aspect of our work, and thus self-examination. What do we really want? If we find our vision is exciting and energizing, we can be sure that our own energies, and even the energies of others, will flow to it and good will come from it.

Many people tend to devote their efforts into avoiding harm rather than creating a positive vision for their work. I cannot emphasize this enough: it is vital that we understand what it is we truly want and live out of that positive possibility if we are to be fulfilled in our life's work.

This principle of *unknown good benefit* has born out time and again in my own life: once I am clear about what I want, it is as if the entire Universe aligns to help! In my own spiritual view, the universe itself is the source of those deepest dreams in the first place, so it makes sense that help arrives once we commit.

You never change things by fighting the existing reality. To change something, build a new model that makes the existing model obsolete.

--Buckminster Fuller

Chapter Five

From Problem To Opportunity

Applied Permaculture Principals

Seeing Problems As Opportunities

In Chapter Four, we introduced the permaculture principles. One of the most transformative of these principles, *the problem is an opportunity*, offers us the ability to fundamentally transform invisible structures by changing our relationship to them. The invisible structures can be societal, cultural, organizational or personal.

How might we begin to see problems as opportunities?

First, we need to consider the conditions under which we face a problem. Some problems come at a time when solving them is particularly difficult or urgent, such as during a crisis. Problems take on greater significance during the most challenging times. During crises, it is clear that action is required and that change is underway or inevitable and even required. When we face significant change, especially when that change includes crises, out of necessity, we often seek out new tools and wisdom.

For example, in my own story described in Chapter One, *the problem* of my depleted energies a decade ago became *an opportunity*, and in fact a mandate, for beneficial change. I could no longer behave in the ways I had been up to that point. Like a plant that had tapped out all of the nutrients in the garden soil, I was struggling. This *problem* seemed insurmountable.

All good gardeners know you must take great care to nurture the garden soil and cultivate health into it. At that critical time in my life, it was as if the soil of my own inner being, was missing certain nutrients to flourish. I longed to just play, and by looking at what was most needed and making some life-giving decisions in that direction, I found the *opportunity*, and a new way forward.

In this case, the opportunity was in discovering the value of exploration and play. In my case, these took the form of culture and spirituality education, art, hobbies, such as pottery and flight training, and rest. This respite from intense work provided me with critical nutrients: knowledge and self-examination, self-care and creativity.

I was ripe for a new direction. After the Masters program at Holy Names University Sophia Center, I finished with a two-week stay at Genesis Farm in New Jersey. The farm experience was a turning point: it brought me more fully into a new way of being, an awareness of the Universe Story and a new cosmology. I became aware of an inner guidance and the fact that I was on a new path.

In retrospect, I realize now that I needed a direct connection with nature and the farm to help it all sink in. I was open to the Genesis Farm experience because Sophia had prepared the soil, encouraging me to trust my intuition. The hands-on experience of gardening and nature at Genesis Farm brought the academic and self-exploration work at the Sophia Center into context.

These two experiences led me to the next step -- participation in a series of regenerative ecological design (permaculture) courses with a talented group of people at both the Center for Solar Living in Hopland and the Earth Activist Training[7].

Permaculture, as a design system based on the above ethics and principles, is also a way to establish, design, manage and improve all efforts made by individuals, families and communities towards a sustainable future.

In my own circumstance, applied permaculture became a positive way forward—I found that I was moving beyond "sustainability" into *co-creating a new and positive reality.* I found permaculture offered me a new way forward.

Permaculture gets us in touch with our human capacity and responsibility to renew depleted and ravaged places. It shows us a way to bring fertility to depleted soils and create better human communities, and people, in the process.

In the years that followed my initial encounter with permaculture, I began integrating permaculture design into the orchard and gardens at Dancing TreePeople Farm[8] and into my role of community leadership in Lake County.

Against the backdrop of global crises, I found it personally empowering to apply these new-found skills in self-sufficiency and community building to my own location, my inner path and the local community. In the process, I was elected to public office and discovered a much broader arena in which to garden.

Seed Balls

One of the more effective concepts in permaculture, as applied to the invisible structures of self-development and community, is the concept of *seed balls*. In permaculture gardening, seed balls are a way to start something new in a devastated place. Conceptually, seed balls represent an approach to very difficult, even devastating, problems.

Seed balls are an ancient way of propagating plants that was reintroduced by natural farmer and father of permaculture, Masanobu Fukuoka. They provide a way to vegetate an area, and are particularly well suited to restoring compacted, barren soils or other disturbed or ravaged places.

Seed balls are a mixture of clay, compost and a guild of seeds—a group of plants that grow together in a *self-sustaining system of mutual support*. Plant *guilds* can be seen as a community—a small self-contained ecosystem.

The clay in the seed ball protects the seeds and keeps them safe until the time is right for germination. The compost provides the initial basic nutrients and microbes to get the seeds started. Seed balls do not require irrigation, they wait patiently for the right conditions: when the rains come, and the soil is warm enough, the seeds will germinate.

How to make seed balls

1. ***Select a guild of seeds.*** These can be native plants or other non-invasive plants. Ideally, select seeds that can support one another—tall grasses might provide a climbing structure for vetches for example. As long as you avoid invasive species, you cannot go wrong, as nature will self-select: the seeds that are well suited for your location will thrive, and others will not.

2. ***Measure equal proportions of compost and clay*** dug from the ground, and mix in your seeds. Then, form them into small balls.

3. ***Set the wet seed balls out to dry.*** Once dried, the seed balls are ready to be broadcast over land that you want to plant. They can be spread at any time of year and they will wait for the ideal time to sprout, when the moisture and temperature conditions are just right.

4. ***Seed balls can be stored*** for later sowing.

Tending the Soul's Garden

Thus seeds balls, by design, are a combination of a self-supporting *guild* community, or set of elemental relationships, protection and patience. All are vital to healing a devastated landscape. The "seed ball" offers us a powerful approach to starting something new:

First, *A seed ball is small and low risk.* Thus, any one small effort can succeed or fail without dire consequence to the whole.

Second, *Seeds are protected and fed.* In personal or community efforts, the seeds can be early projects or ideas, or new life energies. Like seeds, these fledgling efforts need protection and support.

Third, *Seed balls are self-contained,* They are, essentially, miniature systems requiring only water and warmth to activate them. They contain all the nutrients needed to survive until established in their hostile landscape.

Finally, *Each seed ball envisions the whole system.* If successful, the system will consist of many seed balls succeeding. Like a small portion of a hologram, the seed ball represents a picture of the whole.

One example of a "seed ball" in our community of Lake County is the *Clarks Island Sustainability Initiative*[9], mentioned in Chapter Two. The Clarks Island Sustainability Initiative is a local public project where a grassroots group of citizens has adopted an island park and is taking on the task of implementing small projects that might have a broader impact for the whole of Lake County. Initial projects included demonstrations of wetland restoration, floating islands to improve water quality, public-sponsored natural building and other visible ecological demonstrations.

Any one project sponsored by the Clarks Island Sustainability Initiative has been low cost and low risk. Over time, this initiative has engaged the entire community: the local business association, neighborhood schools, local tribes, local government and community members. It has already sparked the imagination of other lakeside communities. Most importantly, the selected projects are demonstrating what works and what doesn't in a fragile lake ecosystem. While all of this is taking place on a small scale, it brings much larger possibilities to the whole county.

Zones

Woven through the principles of perma-culture described in Chapter Four is the concept of efficient use of energy. Principles such as: energy cycling, least change for the greatest effect, relative location, stacking functions, even working with and within nature all have, at their core, the idea of conserving energy, *particularly personal energy or time*. In fact, our own time is a non-renewable resource, and thus one of the most valuable.

With this in mind, permaculture designers approach the design of any system using five *zones*. These zones one through five, are designated based upon how much attention the items placed in the zones require, with Zone One being the most proximate and Zone five being the most distant.

In a physical system, such as a homestead, these Zones might look like this:

Zone One: Garden plants that need daily tending, such as herbs and kitchen vegetables used daily.

Zone Two: Compost bins, vegetable gardens requiring less frequent tending, small animals, chickens.

Zone Three: Orchard areas, ponds, and crops requiring one harvest.

Zone Four: Grazing land, wood lot.

Zone Five: Untouched wild land.

In such a system, the human energy is conserved because the items requiring daily attention are close by. Energies can be further cycled or conserved by the relative location of the elements within such a system.

When considering our personal well-being, zones one through five can be a decision-making construct for external items requiring prioritization, with the most important items requiring the most attention in Zone One. In addition, the most significant daily self-awareness and self-care zone needs to be added. This is the zone that fuels all the others and requires special emphasis: Zone Zero.

Zone Zero

When first engaging in the practice of permaculture, the sheer volume of information can be overwhelming. Humans have been observing the natural world from the beginning, and initially wisdom was passed along in oral traditions through myths and stories. Later forms of knowledge and wisdom were written and housed in libraries. Some forms of wisdom, including nature-based, intuitive and indigenous wisdom, have been largely forgotten or ignored in modern times.

How might we of the modern age reengage without becoming overwhelmed? How might we discover and rediscover all forms of human and natural wisdom? Even the summary information in this book can seem a bit bewildering: three main intentions, three root practices, thirteen principles for engaging intentions, and now multiple zones. Central to creating abundance, through the careful cultivating of our own energies, is starting with what permaculture designers call *Zone Zero*.

To cultivate abundance and gifts in any or all of the other zones, whether they be our family in zone one, our jobs in zone two, or our community, nation or world in zones three, four, and five, we must start by enriching the soil of Zone Zero, also known as our own inner life. Next, in Chapter Six, we touch into the types of nutrients that might enrich the soil of this Zone Zero.

If we want to transform any structures, garden, farm, or community, this is how we engage.

Don't ask what the world needs. Ask what makes you come alive, and go do it. Because what the world needs are people who have come alive.

--Howard Thurman

Chapter Six

Soul Nutrients

Presence

Are you working the soil? Or is the soil working you?

–Benjamin Fahrer

Transformation requires active engagement, but also a living spirit nourished and infused with life. While the action or engagement can often be initiated out of anger, we can only transform structures when we act out of a deeper place, out of love or greater sense of purpose. A great shift of human mind and spirit is required to abandon consumption, acquisition and our own individual contribution to war and destruction of Earth.

Think about those in your life that have truly changed you. Aren't we changed more by who people *are* than by what they do? There seems to be a quality of *being* required to pursue positive change in our world.

How, then, might we discover this place of truth and life within ourselves? If we aren't taught how to discover this inner authority in school or in business or even in community organizing, how might we find the wisdom to create life and abundance for ourselves?

Above all, if we are to become people of transformation, we must pursue self-knowledge, wisdom and an interior life. Without knowing what truly motivates us, we cannot stay focused and centered in the face of that which affronts us.

Beauty, Creativity and Play

When I am working on a problem,
I never think about beauty... but when I
have finished, if the solution is not beauti-
ful, I know it is wrong.

–Buckminster Fuller

The gifts of appreciating and creating beauty or simply engaging in play have this in common: these gifts act as a gateway to another realm, a place where our soul lives. This point of being in the moment with appreciation, joy and spontaneity frees us to imagine, to dream and to create.

This is a place of mystery, and while we are there, we transform our world and ourselves. Beauty, creativity and play have the capacity to lift the darkness of despair and create something new and alive.

{128}

Cultivating play in the garden is as simple as cultivating life in the soil without any intention of production or outcome. Play allows us to create beauty—we see with different eyes and place elements creatively, playfully and beautifully. And, while neither play nor beauty are the primary design criteria in most permaculture gardens, the gardens are often seen as whimsical and are almost always quite beautiful.

Wisdom

Seeking information is a valuable principle for the permaculture garden. Similarly, seeking self-information and wisdom, is valuable when applying permaculture to inner life or invisible structures. Awareness emerges by observing nature and from within ourselves; from our own inner knowing. We cultivate inner awareness through a variety of spiritual practices, through regular meditation or simply by allowing ourselves to just *be*.

Thomas Berry writes of *The Fourfold Wisdom*[11]: the wisdom of indigenous people, the wisdom of women, the wisdom of science, and the wisdom of classical faith traditions. In doing so, he notes that in our current modern-day culture, we tend to rely on scientific wisdom over intuitive and natural wisdom. The cultivation of the previously forsaken sources of wisdom is vital to our collective future.

Like a garden soil that is lacking in specific nutrients, it is important that we reclaim and restore all available wisdom. We must seek balance in order to cultivate a new abundance in our lives. To engage in the Great Work of restoring and renewing our world, we must start with the soil of our own spirit. Sources of wisdom are vital for the collective human spirit. In the practice of soul-tending permaculture, these sources of wisdom become the nutrients for growth.

Feminine Wisdom

So much of human awakening, in both women and men, is aided by the self-discovery of the strong, positive feminine energy. This is the wild and unstructured creative force, playful and powerful. A deep wisdom is contained within our own stories as women, mothers, sojourners, and those of others whose stories have touched our own. Many women recall the struggle to come home to themselves.

Intuition and inner knowing are examples of this form of deep wisdom.

The Wisdom of Science

Emerging science offers a deeper understanding of our creation story and the wonder of the natural world and the universe. The Universe Story, particularly the role of fundamental forces and the Universe's ongoing evolution into greater complexity and differentiation, offers us insights into our own story and our individual evolution as human beings. The dynamics at the moment of creation offers key insights into mystery as well as our own growing consciousness. We turn to the wisdom of science to teach us how things work together, the magic of living systems, chaos theory, quantum physics, fractals, genetic science and holographic theory. By appreciating the intelligence, elegance and complexity of the natural world, we engage the world of science and its special type of wisdom. Examining the early universe at that instant of the primordial flaring forth, we find that science meets mysticism and both contemplate the source of creation as well as the emergence, nature and role of the Universe's fundamental forces. Through the wisdom of science, we can view ourselves as creatures: our story of evolution and transformation as a part of the universe story itself.

The Wisdom of Indigenous Humans

One of the ways indigenous wisdom and story emerges today is in symbols, dreams and archetypes. In this way, unconscious reality comes into consciousness, hidden becomes apparent, destruction transforms into new life. Indigenous wisdom reminds us that the natural world is enchanting and sacred, and that we are a part of it.

By acknowledging the role of synchronicity, of archetypal and personal energies and subtlety, we awaken to claim inner authority and life.

Archetypes in the human psyche are essentially relational patterns that have been observed over the course of human history. Just as attention to relationships and patterns is vital in the permaculture garden, archetypal symbols and relationships are particularly powerful in cultivating our inner garden.

The Wisdom of Classical Religious and Spiritual Traditions.

Through the mystics of all faith traditions, and the discipline of traditional ritual and spiritual practice, we seek our own path to the sacred. Sacramental life, paschal mystery, and the very root of many faith traditions; compassion for the plight of others, offers a way to make sense of suffering and hold true to the promise of new life. Our traditions can help us see creation as sacred, and to pay attention to the call of mystery in our lives. To integrate the best of our own faith tradition connects us to those who have walked the path before us.

Imagination

Imagination is the eye of the soul.

--Joseph Joubert

Using our imagination is both fun and necessary to the garden of our soul—and to our long-term human survival. Imagination is one of the most important tools in permaculture: and, along with information, can be a limiting factor in any design. Cultivating imagination is critical in any circumstance that a permaculture designer faces, whether it be in the garden or the community, or in envisioning our own future.

Imagination is also vital as we face the difficulties related to human and biosphere survival on planet earth. Our culture's collective approach to our problems today shows an appalling lack of imagination. Most noteably, we seem to lack the imagination of the positive, just and sustainable outcomes we wish to create.

In his essay: *Twelve Understandings Concerning the Ecozoic Era*, Thomas Berry wrote: "Earth is a one-time sacred endowment in the unfolding of the Universe."[12] Imagination is required to truly understand and to live this reality.

Imagine what it would be like if all humans on the planet were to *see Earth as our most important relationship*. How would we behave differently if we believed this were true? If Earth was considered the first and primary relationship for each of us, how would our education change, our recreation, our rituals, and our livelihood? What if we were all to suddenly see Earth as sacred? How might we see each hill, rock, stream and creature? What if we saw our primary role as one of creating, or more precisely *co-creating*, abundance and beauty? What ways would we find to enter into the sacred mystery of Creation?

Imagine what it would be like if all this human creativity and talent were suddenly awakened to the cause of reforming or returning human interrelationship with each other and our planet home. Issues of justice, which are fundamentally relational, are directly dependent upon us getting this first planetary relationship right.

Imagination may be one of the most important soul nutrients, and cultivating it is one of the aspects of permaculture as applied to human systems.

Gratitude

The heart of our difficulty may well be a lack of gratitude.

Essential to the practice of permaculture is the cultivation and practice of gratitude. Gratitude is a gift, both to give it and to receive it is a blessing. Counting our blessings allows us to *Return the Surplus* with joy and a sense of fulfillment. By creating abundance, we understand and know that there is more than enough for everyone. Gratitude is a gift and cultivating gratitude is a *choice*.

And all around us, the need for gratitude is clear. As a species, we may well be as disconnected from the consequences of our actions as almost any generation of humans has ever been. Up to this moment, we have been a people asleep, in what seems to be some form of insanity, or deep denial and disconnection.

The natural world is responding to our ir-responsibility in a variety of ways, including increasing rates of cancer. These illnesses that we biopsy and irradiate and remove, and sadly often to which we succumb, are but a symptom of a greater problem--many are awakening to the insanity with a chilling realization that we have taken for granted the most basic of gifts: clean water, wholesome food and a world that accepts and transforms the waste we create. The path we are on leads to ruin; we will consume ourselves -- soon enough, *unless we choose not to.*

The heart of our difficulty may well be a lack of gratitude. To begin, we can cultivate gratitude in our own lives. In doing so, we become more aware of the abundance in our lives and focus on that rather than what we lack. Over time, the change in our focus creates a change within us. It is as if by focusing on abundance, we create and attract abundance to us!

So, take a moment to give thanks: for the miracle of our own lives, of the amazing life all around us; for the precious gifts that allow us to be: food, water, air; for friendship and relationship; for all those who bear the painful burden of our excess, be they human or not; for the simple gifts that mean so much and were given to so many of us for free: health and sunshine and love; and of course for life itself –which can be so very fragile. Perhaps our love and gratitude will help us create a new way forward.

Our Sense of Place

On a typical summer day on our farm, we sauté vegetables from the garden in locally produced olive oil along with farm fresh eggs, seasoned with our own garden basil. We collect vegetables from our kitchen garden and eat fruit fresh from our trees. Our family takes pride in these local meals and delights in how delicious they can be.

In the United States, food travels, on average, 1500 miles from producer to table, requiring huge amounts of fossil fuels both to grow it and deliver it. Most of this food at our Lake County table traveled less than 100 feet. And it tastes a lot better. Everything is flavorful and colorful and nutritious. Northern California small farms are so bountiful... as sunlight streams in through the kitchen window, I often think: *it can't get much better than this*. What better way to cultivate ones own spirit and heal Earth at the same time?

What have you eaten in the last 24 hours? Where did your food come from? Do you know your farmer? What is the source of your water?

If we grow our own food and share with others, we already know how important it is to live locally. By buying local food, we support our farmers and economy right where we live. This simple act of eating locally is one way of supporting a sustainable way forward, in harmony and community with Earth and all her beings.

Compassion

*We didn't invent compassion, but it's flow-
ing through us—or it could. The phase change
that we're in seems, to me, to depend upon
that comprehensive compassion unfurling in
the human species.* [13]

--Brian Swimme

Compassion may be one of the more powerful "soul" nutrients enabling growth and transformation—in all aspects of permaculture. Classical spiritual traditions have offered paths to cultivating compassion and there are many good books on that subject, so I will not elaborate here. However, it must be said that compassion allows us to see things from another point of view and it is a means by which we can live our ethical intentions. Cultivating compassion starts with self-compassion: understanding what motivates us, suspending self-judgment and negative self-talk, and allowing ourselves to be present to whatever we are experiencing in the moment. The act of noticing, of paying attention and of experiencing gives us the information we need to make decisions and choices about where to spend our energies. This ultimately leads us to take action that transforms our own internal structures and, in doing so, the world around us. Like gratitude, compassion is a gift, and thus both to offer and to receive compassion is a blessing. Paradoxically, by cultivating compassion, we also experience the pain of our world and the pain of others while at the same time living life more fully.

Cultivating compassion, as a practice, creates the conditions for positive change. Again, the *decision* to cultivate compassion, and the powerful practice of *noticing but not judging*, in itself creates good benefit.

Many communities around the globe are endorsing the International Charter for Compassion as a way to bring awareness to their own community. The Charter for Compassion is a worldwide effort launched by noted religious scholar Karen Armstrong and elaborated in her book *Twelve Steps to a Compassionate Life*. The Charter for Compassion document, now translated into more than 30 languages, transcends religious, ideological and national difference, and is supported by many leading thinkers from many traditions.

Many local communities, such as our own Lake County, have endorsed the following Charter for Compassion and are promoting the awareness of compassion and the cultivation of community compassion through action.

The Text of the Charter for Compassion is reprinted here and can also be found online at www.charterforcompassion.org.

The Charter for Compassion[14]

"The principle of compassion lies at the heart of all religious, ethical and spiritual traditions, calling us always to treat all others as we wish to be treated ourselves. Compassion impels us to work tirelessly to alleviate the suffering of our fellow creatures, to dethrone ourselves from the center of our world and put another there, and to honor the inviolable sanctity of every single human being, treating everybody, without exception, with absolute justice, equity and

respect.

It is also necessary in both public and private life to refrain consistently and empathically from inflicting pain. To act or speak violently out of spite, chauvinism, or self-interest, to impoverish, exploit or deny basic rights to anybody, and to incite hatred by denigrating others—even our enemies—is a denial of our common humanity. We acknowledge that we have failed to live compassionately and that some have even increased the sum of human misery in the name of religion.

We therefore call upon all men and women ~ to restore compassion to the center of morality and religion ~ to return to the ancient principle that any interpretation of scripture that breeds violence, hatred or disdain is illegitimate ~ to ensure that youth are given accurate and respectful information about other traditions, religions and cultures ~ to encourage a positive appreciation of cultural and religious diversity ~ to cultivate an informed empathy with the suffering of all human beings, even those regarded as enemies.

We urgently need to make compassion a

clear, luminous and dynamic force in our polarized world. Rooted in a principled determination to transcend selfishness, compassion can break down political, dogmatic, ideological and religious boundaries. Born of our deep interdependence, compassion is essential to human relationships and to a fulfilled humanity. It is the path to enlightenment, and indispensible to the creation of a just economy and a peaceful global community."

Awareness of Attraction

What draws you? Permaculture designers begin to see activities in which they engage as a path to abundance. From moment to moment, they ask the question: "To what am I drawn?" "What is calling to me in this moment?"

The practice of permaculture is aligned with what Thomas Berry calls The *Great Work of Our Time.* The Universe Story offers us an integrated spirituality; namely that of interconnectedness and common shared origin, and a way forward aligned with the principles and ways of nature herself.

By aligning our own curiosity and positive energies, and by working on that which most interests us, however small, we, in effect are co-creating and co-evolving with the Universe. We are like a hologram, reflecting the beauty of The Whole.

How does this work in everyday life? If we find that we are no longer energetic about the work in front of us, then we tend to force our energies to engage, or even participate. If this happens for too many days in a row, then perhaps we need to reassess our path.

Or perhaps we need to attend to something else at that moment on that particular day. A useful question might be: "What is calling to (or blocking) my energy right now?" An overdue assignment? An unreturned phone call? By paying attention, one develops a level of trust in an inner wisdom that soon comes naturally. To engage fully, we must notice the state of our internal energies at any given time and tend to them in the moment. Sometimes this can be as simple as scheduling time on a later date for completing an assignment or by giving ourselves permission to let go of something on our to-do list.

There are many challenges in transforming our culture into one that is more mutually beneficial to the planet Earth. If we begin by nurturing the soil of our spirit, and pay attention to supplying the needed nutrients on a regular basis, we will not only have the energy to engage in the work, we will thrive.

In the immense story of the Universe, that so many dangerous moments have been navigated successfully is some indication that the Universe is for us rather than against us. We need only summon these forces to our support in order to succeed.[10]

–*Thomas Berry*

Chapter Seven

A Way Forward

Completing the Circle

At the beginning of this book, we learned that we must start with our intention, specifically our *ethical intention*, if we wish to create a better world. We also learned that we can easily be discouraged and overwhelmed by the sheer magnitude of the work ahead and we learned that nurturing our own spirit, and cultivating our growth and evolution is part of that work.

If we want to live in harmony with the planet, to accept our position as a part of the natural system rather than a consumer (taker) of Earth's gifts, then an internal shift is required--a change in our way of being. Much of what we have been taught about ourselves--how to be happy, how to survive, how to relate--must necessarily change. Despite what we have been taught by popular culture since infancy, we do not need more things to make us happy. In fact, paradoxically, the more we have, the more elusive happiness becomes. Yet, despite the fact that heroes are rewarded and individualism is worshiped in our culture, the most important gifts in the next few decades may well be our relationships with neighbors and the cultivation of local community.

Why is this? Because no one person can possibly have all the skills or resources or tools or creativity or time to be fully sustainable on his or her own. Even if we had unlimited resources we could devote to this project, we would not have the time or strength working alone. More importantly, the vision of such a life is unappealing and the system itself unstable. We need a life-giving and sustaining vision, a spiritual sustenance, in order to let go of the false promises ingrained so deeply within us. As it turns out, our ability to forge relationships and our own creativity are probably our most important individual gifts.

At the same time, The Universe Story, the story of 13.7 billion years of physical evolution and growing spiritual consciousness, is being translated and made available to all segments of the human community, and celebrated as our common origin. This story is quickly becoming a functional cosmology for our entire human family. We find ourselves a part of a story, one where we all have common origins and where we all are part of a whole living system on planet Earth.

Permaculture is a way of applying that new cosmology to our surroundings and ourselves, both practically and spiritually. Permaculture offers us an integrated way of living within this emerging story.

By continually observing, imitating and co-creating with the natural world, we soon find ourselves *living* permaculture. In this way, we behave as a part of our natural world instead of apart from it. *We become indigenous to the plant Earth once again*, our daily work is the same as our spirituality, and the same as our ideology— all consistent with our cosmology.

Signs of Change

"We must turn all our resources to repairing the natural world, and train all our young people to help. They want to. We need to give them this last chance to create forests, soils, clean waters, clean energies, secure communities, stable regions, and to know how to do it from hands-on experience."[16]

As I harvest the first of our organic vegetables and contemplate the season ahead, I drink in the beauty of the landscape around me at my home in Lake County. I am grateful for all I have been given. From the land and trees, to the community of life and the community of people. We have all that we need for the times ahead. My hope and dream is that we accept all that is entrusted to us and make it better for generations to come.

We look to the future and our relationship with the next generation. We face a stark choice: a path of fear, cynicism and despair, or one of renewal, restoration and of co-creating abundance for the future. Our young people are already keenly aware of the dire state of the world, with messages from media that lead to desolation. It is our task to offer a positive path forward even as we help them, and ourselves, through the grief and despair over what we have inherited.

The solution to global difficulties lies within Earth herself: in our human family finding harmony and cooperation with and within her systems, not in competition with them, and in our creativity.

Today, in permaculture design courses around the globe, many young adults are learning the techniques of renewal. These young people are from all educational and cultural backgrounds and ethnicities. What they have in common is the desire to learn skills that will help renew and restore damaged places, create healthy soil and grow food, and create resilient communities.

Permaculture skills and philosophies are an important way to survive both physically and spiritually: creating abundance in these times and in the years of transition and restoration ahead. For the young, corporate jobs will become scarce, and far less satisfying. Permaculture courses offer not only skills for ongoing sustainability, but also for regenerating our soils and depleted Earth… and our depleted human spirit. To quote Bill Mollison, one of the principal founders of permaculture:

> *"In designing with nature, rather than against it, we can create landscapes that operate like healthy natural systems, where energy is conserved, wastes are recycled and resources are abundant."* --Bill Mollison[17]

Our youth want and need both a positive way forward and an understanding of their part in making it happen. The practice of permaculture offers this and more. Perhaps Earth and the ways of the natural world will help us find our way.

What did you do, once you knew? [15]

--Drew Dellinger

Resources

Armstrong, K. (2010). *Twelve Steps to a Compassionate Life*. New York, NY: Alfred A. Knopf Publisher.

Berry, T. (2009, January 1). *Twelve Understandings Concerning the Ecozoic Era*: Center for Ecozoic Studies: http://www.ecozoicstudies.org/statements/twelve-understandings-concerning-the-ecozoic-era

Berry, T. (1988). *The Dream of the Earth*. San Francisco, CA: Sierra Club Books.

Berry, T. (1999). *The Great Work*. New York, NY: The Bell Tower.

Berry, T., & Swimme, B. (1994). *The Universe Story*. San Francisco, CA: Harper Collins.

Brown, M. Y., & Macy, J. (1998). *Coming Back to Life*. Ontario, Canada: New Society Publishers.

Earth Charter: http://www.earthcharteri-
naction.org/.

Fukuoka, M. (1978). *The One-Straw
Revolution.* (C. Pearce, T. Kurosawa, & L.
Korn, Trans.) Tokyo:
Rodale Press.

Hawken, P. (2009, May 3). *Paul Hawken
Univeristy of Portland Commencement
Speech.* Retrieved March 3, 2011, from
Paul Hawken: http://www.paulhawken.
com/UofP_Commencement.pdf.

Hemenway, T. (2000). *Gaia's Garden,
A Guide to Home Scale Permaculture.*
White River Junction, VT: Chelsea
Green Publishing Company.

Holmgren, D. (2002). *Permaculture:
Principles and Pathways Beyond Sustainability.* Hepburn, Victoria 3461, Australia: Holmgren Design Services.

Mollison, B. (1988). *PERMACULTURE:
A Designers' Manual.* Sisters Creek,
Tasmania 7325, Australia: Tagari Publi-
cations.

Rushing, D. (2010, December 1). *Welcome to Dancing TreePeople Farm*. Retrieved February 28, 2011, from Dancing TreePeople Farm: www.dancingtreepeople.com.

Shepherd, L. J. (2007, May 1). *Song of Waitaha, review for New Zealand Geographic*. Retrieved March 3, 2011, from Academia.edu: http://ciis.academia.edu/LindaJeanShepherd/Papers/137503/Song_of_Waitaha_review_for_New_Zealand_Geographic.

Starhawk (2005). *The Earth Path: Grounding Your Spirit in the Rhythms of Nature*. New York, NY: Harper Collins.

Swimme, B. (1996). *The Hidden Heart of the Cosmos*. New York, NY: Orbis Books.

Notes

1. Shepherd, L. J. (2007, May/June). Song of Waitaha, review for New Zealand Geographic. Retrieved March 3, 2011, from Academia.edu: http://ciis.academia.edu/Linda-JeanShepherd/Papers/137503/Song_of_Waitaha_review_for_New_Zealand_Geographic.

2. Berry, T. (1999). The Great Work. New York, NY: The Bell Tower, pp. 3.

3. Adapted from Mollison, B. (1988). PERMACULTURE: A Designers' Manual. Sisters Creek, Tasmania 7325, Australia: Tagari Publications. p. 2.

4. Mollison, 1988, p. 1.

5. Berry, T. 1999, pp. 201

6. Fukuoka, M. (1978). The One-Straw Revolution. (C. Pearce, T. Kurosawa, & L. Korn, Trans.) Tokyo: Rodale Press. p.119

7. Earth Activist Training website: http://www.earthactivisttraining.org.

8. Dancing TreePeople Farm website: http://www.dancing-treepeople.com.

9. Clarks Island Sustainability Initiative is available online at http://www.clarksisland.net.

10. Berry, T. 1999, p 201.

11. Berry, T. 1999, pp. 176-195.

12. Berry, T. (2009, January 1). Twelve Understandings Concerning the Ecozoic Era. Retrieved January 15, 2011, from Center for Ecozoic Studies: http://www.ecozoicstudies. org/statements/twelve-understandings-concerning-the-ecozoic-era

13. Retrieved April 11, 2011, from EnlightenNext Magazine: Comprehensive Compassion, An Interview with Brian Swimme,, by Susan Bridle. http://www.enlightennext.org/ magazine/j19/swimme.asp?page=2.

14. Retrieved March 23, 2011, from International Charter for Compassion: http://www.charterforcompassion.org.

15. Dellinger, D. (2010). Love Letter to the Milky Way. Mill Valley, CA: Planetize the Movement Press, p.1.

16. Mollison, B. (1988). PERMACULTURE: A Designers' Manual. Sisters Creek, Tasmania 7325, Australia: Tagari Publications.

17. Mollison, B. and Slay, Rita Mia, 1994. Introduction to Permaculture, New Edition. Tyalgum, NSW: Tagari Publications. p. 72.

Index

49528552R00115

Made in the USA
San Bernardino, CA
22 August 2019